NATURE'S WAY TO BATTLE THE BLUES

No one should have to live with depression. Unfortunately, powerful prescription drugs like Prozac, Paxil and Effexor can be almost as intolerable, not to mention expensive. Happily, nature has provided a whole range of gentler antidepressants: St. John's Wort, 5-hydroxytryptophan, S-adenosylmenthionine, tyrosine, phenylalanine and folic acid, among many others. Considerable research indicates that these herbs, biochemical and nutrients can often counteract clinical depression as efficiently and effectively as prescription drugs, but with fewer side effects and a more modest price tag.

ABOUT THE AUTHOR

Syd Baumel is a Canadian writer who specializes in natural health and medicine. He is the author of three books, among them the Doubleday Health Book Club Main Alternate *Dealing with Depression Naturally* (Keats, 1995) and *Serotonin* (Keats, 1997). His many articles have appeared in such publications as *Alive, The Aquarian, Bestways, Energy Times, Health, Natural Life* and *The New Age Connection.* Also an editor, record reviewer and amateur artist and composer, Baumel lives in Winnipeg, Manitoba.

To find out more about Syd Baumel's other books, see: <www.escape.ca/~sgb/depression.html> and <www.escape.ca/~sgb/serotonin.html>.

Natural Antidepressants

Tried and true remedies from nature's pharmacy

by Syd Baumel
Author of *Dealing with Depression Naturally* and *Serotonin*

KEATS PUBLISHING
LOS ANGELES
NTC/Contemporary Publishing Group

Natural Antidepressants is not intended as medical advice. Its intent is solely informational and educational. Please consult a health professional should the need for one be indicated.

NATURAL ANTIDEPRESSANTS

ISBN: 0-87983-900-7

Printed in the United States of America

Keats Good Health Guides™ are published by
Keats Publishing
a division of the NTC/ Contemporary Publishing Group
4255 West Touhy Avenue
Lincolnwood, Illinois 60646-1975

Full catalog and ordering information: www.keats.com

04 05 06 07 RCP 5 4 3 2

Contents

INTRODUCTION

As I write this in the summer of 1998, the treatment of depression by a humble health food store supplement has for the first time ever become a widely accepted practice. Celebrated in the media as nature's answer to Prozac, the herb St. John's Wort is now used by millions of people to relieve their depression at a fraction of the cost—in dollars and side effects—of today's user-friendliest drugs. Suddenly the idea that nature's pharmacy stocks antidepressants on its rustic shelves seems not so far-fetched.

Luckily, St. John's Wort (SJW) is not the only one. Other drugs or supplements work much better for some people. In fact, there are so many worthwhile natural antidepressants that a book of this size cannot hope to reasonably accommodate them all. Instead, what we'll do here is focus on a select few—the best and brightest pills that you can pop in your mouth like Paxil or Prozac. (We'll briefly review a variety of other natural approaches in the final section.)

DEFINING DEPRESSION

Depression comes in many different forms—more, undoubtedly, than even the ever-expanding classification system of modern psychiatry has yet to encompass. So I won't ask you to try to measure up to checklists of symptoms that may already be outdated by the time you read this. In the end, whether your depression has lasted years or days, whether it makes you feel like you're in hell or just in a momentary limbo, whether you've lost your appetite or just can't stop eating, whether you wake up in a panic before dawn or sleep like a corpse until noon, whether you're an apathetic slug or an hysterical wreck, whether you're mired in self-pity or seething with hostility, whether you can't stop crying or you're stone cold dry—if you *feel* depressed (unhappily stuck in a rut by the side of the road), you *are,* by your own very important definition, depressed.

But is depression your primary problem?

Undiagnosed physical conditions can masquerade as depression (Gold, 1987; Baumel, 1995). What seems on the surface to be just another "chemical imbalance" or "nervous breakdown" may actually be a complication of an underactive thyroid gland, a reaction to brain-toxic workplace chemicals, an early symptom of diabetes, an adverse drug reaction or the tip of the iceberg of any one of a hundred or so other disorders. And if you're not just depressed, but have other psychobehavioral symptoms, such as panic attacks, phobias, substance abuse, delusions or hallucinations, you may have another psychiatric disorder—perhaps primary, perhaps secondary, to the depression—that puts a different spin on your treatment possibilities. There are times when it's good to see a doctor, and this could be one of them.

ST. JOHN'S WORT: PSYCHIATRY'S HERBAL EPIPHANY

In the early nineties, the world acquired a new concept—antidepressant wonder drug—and a new name—*Prozac*. As the nineties draw to a close, the world has acquired another concept—antidepressant wonder supplement—and *St. John's Wort* (SJW) is its name.

Media hype—as with Prozac before it—may have created exaggerated expectations for SJW; but, still, SJW is at least as good a natural, first-line therapy for depression as any other. Indeed, no antidepressant supplement can claim as many favorable studies and relatively safe patient-years of use.

In 1996, the prestigious *British Medical Journal* published a landmark meta-analysis of 23 scientifically well-controlled trials of SJW for depression (Linde et al., 1996). A total of 1,757 patients, most of them suffering from clinically mild to moderately severe cases of the blues, received SJW, low doses of an antidepressant medication, or a placebo, usually for 4 to 8 weeks. Overall, SJW performed over 150 percent better than the dummy placebo pills and 10 percent better than the drugs. SJW users even reported fewer side effects than patients on placebo, suggesting that the herb quelled rather than fueled the background noise of people's everyday aches and angsts. In a subsequent review, the highest, most commonly recommended dosage of SJW wiped out or substantially relieved depression in 75 percent of the patients (Nordfors and Hartvig, 1997).

In Germany, from which most of this research has emanated, doctors have taken to prescribing SJW more often than any other antidepressant—you-know-Whozac included. There were nearly 3 million prescriptions in 1993 alone

(Linde et al., 1996). In 1996, SJW mania hit North America. Even the National Institute of Mental Health felt compelled to initiate its own major multicenter trial. On Internet newsgroups and mailing lists, no natural antidepressant—and possibly no antidepressant drug—generates as much talk. Of the SJW users who have shared their impressions on these interactive electronic bulletin boards or privately with me, some, inevitably, have found no relief, but most have noted mild to spectacular improvements. Some have hailed the herb as "a lifesaver," "a miracle" or "a godsend." Here are some of their tributes:

"St. John's Wort has been like a miracle for me. . . . I am constantly thinking to myself, 'Is this how other people have always felt? How wonderful!' "

"My depression's GONE. Till a few months ago, I'd sit alone at break and wonder if everyone else were just acting differently than they felt. . . . I'm a different person inside now!"

"All I know is that I've tried nine antidepressants . . . they've all made me very sick. SJW doesn't."

"[SJW] pulled me out of a six- to seven-year bout of anxiety and depression in two weeks. . . . I've got my life back. . . ."

"The best I've felt [after trying eight different antidepressant drugs, alone and sometimes in combination] is with 10 mg Prozac + St. John's Wort. . . . I just plain feel better and sleep way better than with 20+ mg Prozac and no St. John's Wort."

"I have been dysthymic [mildly depressed] for as long as I can remember. . . . [At the height of a severe depression] I was borderline suicidal when I started SJW in May 1997. Last week, less than six months. on SJW, my p-doc [psychiatrist] released me and declared me a "normie". . . . I tried going off of it this week, and after three days I was slipping fast."

". . . It has diminished my depressive symptoms [unsatisfactorily treated with drugs till then] effectively, quickly, but almost imperceptibly. . . . [T]he blackness is gone, but everything else remains as it was. . . . [I]t has worked for me in a way I never thought possible. . . ."

"[I]t keeps me from feeling and acting like a raving bitch all the time. My kids want to thank that St. John fellow."

How *Does* St. John's Wort Work?

Until recently, SJW's mechanism of action seemed clear. Early research indicated that a prominent active ingredient named *hypericin* was a *monoamine oxidase inhibitor* (MAOI), just like the MAOI drugs used to treat depression. But later studies showed that therapeutic doses of SJW have too weak a MAOI effect to single-handedly relieve depression. As if on cue, new research began pointing to other possible mechanisms: suppression of excessive cortisol release by the adrenal glands (a sign of severe stress and severe depression); mimicking the calming neurotransmitter GABA, just like Valium and other benzodiazepine tranquilizers; and finally—in typical antidepressant drug fashion—inhibiting the neuronal reuptake of three key mood-related neurotransmitters: serotonin, norepinephrine and dopamine. In one test-tube study, SJW seemed to perform a medley of antidepressant drugs' greatest hits: it inhibited serotonin and NE reuptake while simultaneously demonstrating very mild MAOI activity. Were SJW a truly strong MAOI, this combination of effects would likely spell catastrophe. Instead, it appears to spell synergy.

IS ST. JOHN'S WORT FOR YOU?

Many would-be experts are quick to "caution" that SJW is not for the severely depressed. A more appropriate caution would be to take this advice with a grain of salt. While clinical trials have concentrated on using SJW to treat clinically mild to moderate depression (which is really quite severe compared with everyday depression), the available research on the effects of SJW on clinically severe depression is encouraging. In a huge drug-monitoring study of SJW, the severely depressed subgroup enjoyed a roughly 40 percent reduction in self-rated depression after just 4 weeks (Bloomfield and McWilliams, 1997). In another study, the severely depressed subgroup saw their depression ratings plummet from an average of 25 to just 9 (very mildly depressed) after 6 weeks (Bloomfield and McWilliams, 1997). And in a recent multicenter trial from Germany where all the patients were severely depressed, 6 weeks on a double dosage of SJW cut depression by nearly 50 percent. The control group, which had received a standard dosage of the venerable tricyclic antidepressant imipramine, fared only slightly better. But with SJW emerging the clear winner in side effects, the researchers concluded that the herb "might be a treatment alternative to the synthetic tricyclic antidepressant imipramine in the majority of severe forms of depressions" (Vorbach et al., 1997).

While it seems that SJW can help no matter how depressed you are or what kind of depression you have, the herb's value for treating psychotic, bipolar and "melancholic" depression (the most intransigent form of severe, nonpsychotic depression) is still little known.

Research suggests SJW can help if you have other symptoms that often go with depression: anxiety (it gradually equaled benzodiazepines in two studies [Bloomfield and McWilliams, 1997], insomnia (though evening doses keep some people awake) and possibly alcoholism, chronic pain, drug dependence, eating disorders, migraine headaches and premenstrual syndrome. Some people (myself included) feel they handle stress better under SJW's influence—and that's certainly an ounce of prevention when it comes to depression.

USING ST. JOHN'S WORT

Some people feel dramatically better almost as soon as they start taking SJW, but more commonly the herb works slowly, over weeks and months, like most antidepressants.

The most commonly recommended dosage of SJW is 900

mg day (usually in three doses) of an SJW extract standardized to contain 0.3 percent hypericin (Bloomfield and McWilliams, 1997). In controlled clinical trials, this dosage has helped 75 percent of depressives compared with just 61 percent on 400 mg or less (Nordfors and Hartvig, 1997). On the other hand, in two huge drug-monitoring studies, the lower dosage actually performed slightly better (Bloomfield and McWilliams, 1997). Consistent with these inconsistencies, some people do poorly on a low dosage and fabulously on a high one, while for others it's vice versa.

SAFETY, SIDE EFFECTS, CAUTIONS AND CONTRAINDICATIONS

Not only has SJW been extraordinarily well-tolerated in clinical trials and drug-monitoring studies, but despite millions of patient-years of use by European men, women and children—including pregnant women—the medical literature so far contains no reports of fatalities, serious side effects or adverse drug interactions (Bloomfield and McWilliams, 1997).

But anecdotally in North America, the SJW experience has been a little rougher around the edges. While nothing really serious has been formally reported, perceived side effects are common. Some of them sound suspiciously like the potentially serious (even lethal) reactions that can occur when strong MAOIs are combined with certain foods (like cheese and chocolate), beverages (like cider and beer), medications (like antidepressant drugs and cold remedies) or supplements (like tyrosine and phenylalanine), leading to the build-up of natural stimulants that can dangerously elevate blood pressure. Headaches (some of them "terrible," "raging," "hellacious," "mind blowing"), stiff neck or pain at the base of the skull, rapid heart beat, palpitations, muscle spasms in the chest, sweatiness, and weird, spaced-out feelings have all been reported by some SJW users, sometimes in combination. A very few people have documented that their blood pressure was high when they had an awful headache after taking SJW while paying no attention to their intake of MAOI-unfriendly foods or medications. More serious is a case anecdotally reported by Mary Arneson, M.D. (1997). Her patient, an elderly woman on a MAOI-unfriendly bladder medication, experienced a hypertensive crisis culminating in a nonfatal hemorrhagic stroke shortly after she started taking SJW.

Reportedly, such reactions are unheard of in Europe (Linde et al., 1996; Bloomfield and McWilliams, 1997). SJW expert Camilla Cracchiolo (1997) suspects this discrepancy may be due to the fact that the best-selling European formulation, *LI 160* (sold here under the brand name Kira), is a pure *alcoholic extract* of SJW. Some North American products may contain stronger MAOIs or other problematic chemicals found only in the whole herb or its oil extract. Significantly, perhaps, the lady who suffered the stroke was taking a whole herb preparation. To play it safe, people taking any brand of SJW might want to monitor their blood pressure, especially if they consume lots of MAOI no-no's (of which there are far too many to list here; please consult your doctor, pharmacist or a good drug reference book) or experience any suspicious symptoms.

Apart from the above reactions, SJW users have also reported other side effects: gastrointestinal upsets, particularly gas, nausea and stomach pains (often relieved by taking SJW with food); headaches (seemingly not hypertensive); muscle fatigue, aches or spasms; extreme drowsiness; insomnia or shallow sleep (especially if SJW is taken in the evening); feeling "wired," restless, nervous, jittery or even mildly manic; breakthrough seizures in an epileptic on dilantin; feelings of hostility, anger, suspicion or alienation; feeling strange, spaced-out, dazed or "in a dream"; absent-mindedness, mental fuzziness; emotional numbness; increasing depression; transient, mild dizzy spells; poor heat tolerance, sweatiness; shortness of breath; diarrhea; swollen feet; and light-induced itch or rash. These reactions are usually mild and often abate with continued use of SJW.

In theory, SJW's effects on serotonin and MAO could trigger a so-called *serotonin syndrome* in sensitive users if the herb is combined with other strongly serotonergic agents, notably MAOI drugs; fenfluramine or dexfenfluramine; Prozac and other SSRIs (selective serotonin reuptake inhibitors); nonselective SRIs (serotonin reuptake inhibitors), like venlafaxine, trazadone and some of the tricyclics; lithium; tryptophan or

5-hydroxytryptophan (5-HTP); and s-adenosylmethionine (SAMe, SAM) or methionine. The serotonin syndrome is an acute attack of twitchy, jerky, shivery, staggering confusion. In very rare cases it escalates to a feverishly fatal pitch. So far, the not uncommon practice of combining SJW with an SSRI hasn't resulted in any reports of such reactions.

TRYPTOPHAN AND 5-HYDROXYTRYPTOPHAN: NATURAL PROZAC AND SON

In the 1980s, if you looked up depression in a medical textbook, you would very often find a favorable mention of tryptophan. The dietary precursor to serotonin—one of the brain's preeminent mood-regulating neurotransmitters—was of questionable efficacy as a solo antidepressant, most experts concluded, but as an adjunct to antidepressant drugs, it was well worth a try.

Today, you won't find tryptophan in many textbooks—at least not as a treatment. An outbreak in 1989 of a severe, sometimes deadly, autoimmune disease called eosinophilia-myalgia syndrome (EMS) was traced to contaminated lots of tryptophan, and supplements of the amino acid have been scarce—whether on the shelves of stores or the pages of textbooks—ever since.

This is unfortunate, for tryptophan's virtues as an antidepressant seem to have been underestimated and its hazards overblown. Prescribed at optimal dosages, the essential nutrient is generally better tolerated than the host of serotonin-boosting drugs that have supplanted it. Indeed, in Canada, "Tryptan" is still prescribed by many doctors for bipolar disorder, depression, and insomnia.

Tryptophan's metabolic offspring, 5-hydroxytryptophan (5-HTP), has suffered more from neglect than disrepute.

Hailed in 1980 by one psychiatrist as the most remarkable antidepressant he had ever known (van Hiele, 1980), research suggests this immediate precursor of serotonin should be a treatment of choice for depression. But, instead, it's a complete unknown for most psychiatrists.

Ever since the dawn of the modern antidepressant era in the 1950s, tryptophan and 5-HTP have seemed born to the role of natural antidepressants. It was then that the two major biochemical theories of depression were first advanced. One postulated that a deficiency of the neurotransmitter norepinephrine lay at the core of depression; the other, that it was a deficiency of serotonin. As the years passed, evidence that tryptophan and serotonin are in short supply in depressed and violently suicidal people mounted steadily. Finally, in the 1990s the antidepressant market was overtaken by a class of drugs that did little or nothing *but* boost serotonin, the SSRIs.

Thirty years earlier, tryptophan had racked up its first successes, beating placebo and equaling antidepressant drugs and even electroconvulsive (shock) therapy in British clinical trials (van Praag, 1981). But while other investigators were usually able to confirm tryptophan's equivalence to drugs, the amino acid didn't deliver in most of its rematches with placebos and ECT (van Praag, 1981). Only as an adjunct to antidepressant drugs—particularly MAOIs—was it a respectably consistent performer.

Poring over the research, some psychiatrists noticed that (for nonbipolar depressives at least) there was a strong trend for tryptophan's failures to occur when it was prescribed at (or hiked up to) a relatively high dosage. Perhaps, they speculated, tryptophan has what is known as a "therapeutic window," that is, high dosages can be as ineffective as low ones (van Praag, 1981; Gelenberg et al., 1982). In roughly half a dozen subsequent trials, most of them utilizing relatively low dosages of tryptophan, this hypothesis has generally been borne out. Modest doses of tryptophan have, for example, proven effective as an alternative or adjunct to bright light for the winter blues (Lam et al., 1997).

There is little ambiguity surrounding 5-HTP's antidepressant effect. What undoubtedly helps is that 5-HTP is just one easily traveled step away from serotonin (unlike tryptophan), with nothing to do but take it. But 5-HTP has another surprising ace up its sleeve (van Praag, 1984): it is taken up not only by serotonergic (serotonin-releasing) neurons but by neurons which secrete norepinephrine (NE) and dopamine (DA), too. Somehow this triggers an increase in NE and DA neurotransmission, no doubt diversifying 5-HTP's antidepressant pharmacological range.

5-HTP has demonstrated its antidepressive mettle in 12 of 16 clinical trials (including some as brief as 1 or 2 weeks), proving itself significantly superior to placebo and tryptophan and/or as effective as antidepressant drugs in most of the dozen or so controlled matches (van Praag, 1981; Poldinger et al., 1991). Unlike St. John's Wort, it has usually been pressed into service for moderately to severely depressed patients, of whom about two in every three have significantly benefited (Poldinger et al., 1991). One psychiatrist found 5-HTP to be like a magic bullet for 44 out of 99 of his most chronically depressed, treatment-resistant patients (Van Hiele, 1980). In its most recent contest—a double-blind, randomized trial involving 69 mostly moderately to severely depressed patients—5-HTP proved marginally more effective and significantly better tolerated than Luvox, an SSRI considered by some to be the most user-friendly drug in its class (Norden, 1995). The study's authors concluded in 1991 that it was high time "5-HTP [be] admitted to the core group of routinely applied antidepressive drugs" (Poldinger et al., 1991).

Hopefully, they weren't holding their breath, for 5-HTP is still awaiting acceptance by the medical mainstream. Public acceptance is another story. Widely available as an over-the-counter supplement, these days 5-HTP is giving even SJW a run for its money. When one mail-order seller (www.life-enhancement.com) surveyed its customers, they expressed a high level of satisfaction with 5-HTP. Among the success stories were an Alaskan who wiped out his winter depression with it (serotonin boosting is the most successful chemical strategy for the condition) and a doctor who called it a wonderful substitute for Paxil, an SSRI that he had previously taken.

ARE TRYPTOPHAN AND 5-HTP FOR YOU?

5-HTP and (less reliably) tryptophan have worked for people with all the major varieties and severities of depression, except possibly psychotic depression (van Praag, 1981). Tryptophan is less likely than other antidepressants to trigger mania in bipolars. Indeed, in Canada, one of Tryptan's official indications is as an adjunct to lithium for combating both phases of the disorder. Tryptophan would also seem less likely to enflame psychotic depression.

Like their cousins the SSRIs, tryptophan and 5-HTP show signs—sometimes fairly **strong** (as indicated by boldface), sometimes relatively preliminary or conflicting—of allaying a wide range of conditions associated with depression (Baumel, 1997): obsessive-compulsive disorder (**tryptophan,** especially as an adjunct to serotonergic drugs), panic disorder (5-HTP) and possibly other anxiety disorders; insomnia (**tryptophan,** 5-HTP); chronic pain (**tryptophan,** 5-HTP), migraine (**5-HTP,** tryptophan) and other headaches (both), and fibromyalgia (**5-HTP**); overeating (including bulimia nervosa), especially "carbohydrate craving" (**both**); premenstrual syndrome (tryptophan); attention deficit hyperactivity disorder (tryptophan); autism (both); substance abuse (including alcoholism and smoking) (both); uncontrollable rage (tryptophan); impulsive behavior disorders, especially involving aggression or violence (tryptophan); schizophrenia (tryptophan); Tourette syndrome (both); Parkinson's disease (both); and dementia, including Alzheimer's disease (both). In a few of these conditions—schizophrenia and Parkinson's, for example—tryptophan and 5-HTP have worsened some people's symptoms, so use with caution.

People with physiological signs of serotonin deficiency, such as a low ratio of plasma tryptophan to other large, neutral amino acids or a low CSF (cerebrospinal fluid) level of 5-HIAA (serotonin's breakdown product), are the best candidates for tryptophan or 5-HTP (Moller et al., 1980; van Praag, 1981).

USING TRYPTOPHAN AND 5-HTP

The antidepressant dose range for tryptophan and 5-HTP seems to be about 1.5 to 6 g and 50 to 600 mg per day, respectively, with most responders requiring 2.5 to 5 grams or 200-300 mg. Good timing with respect to food intake (as described below) and the use of adjunctive serotonin-boosting supplements or drugs (SAM, SJW, SSRIs.) can markedly lower the required dosage.

Both tryptophan and 5-HTP appear to have a therapeutic window. At very high doses, tryptophan actually becomes a downer, capable of relieving acute mania. 5-HTP may even have a "therapeutic piano window": "In some patients the effect of l-5-HTP hinges on 10-25 mg/day more or less," observes one very fastidious prescriber (van Hiele, 1980). To avoid overshooting this sliver of a window, he slowly builds each patient's dose up by just 10 mg every 3 to 7 days. When the right dosage is found (usually 200 to 300 mg), marked improvement often occurs within days (van Hiele, 1980; Poldinger et al., 1991). One-size-fits-all dosages in the 200 to 300 mg range have been the norm in 5-HTP's many successful clinical trials.

THE SAFETY ISSUE

The results of numerous independent investigations have left few, if any, authorities doubting that the crippling, sometimes deadly outbreak in 1989 of EMS in thousands of tryptophan users was entirely due to contamination by a major manufacturer, Showa Denko of Japan. Unfortunately, that's not the whole story. There have also been sporadic reports of serious EMS-like syndromes or symptoms—eosinophilia, skin disorders, life-threatening pulmonary hypertension—in people using other sources of tryptophan—and *5-HTP*. In one study, while six of 17 people with the rare EMS-like syndrome of eosinophilic fasciitis (Shulman's syndrome) had been using contaminated Showa Denko tryptophan, five others had only used other sources of tryptophan (Blauvelt and Falanga, 1991). In another report, a Showa Denko-like impurity was identified in the 5-HTP used by three people exhibiting EMS-like signs and symptoms (Michelson et al., 1994).

Contamination is not the only concern. Tryptophan and

5-HTP have normal metabolic products which, in excess, can be harmful in ways reminiscent of EMS (fibrotic skin and lung diseases) and in other ways, too (AIDS dementia, bladder tumors, cataracts, Parkinson's disease) (Sourkes, 1983).

Sadly, it would seem that there is something inherently dangerous about tryptophan and 5-HTP. It's an elusive danger, because in many millions of patient-years of use (tryptophan was immensely popular in the seventies and eighties), only a few dozen severe reactions have been reported. But other cases may have gone unattributed. One unsettling possibility is that the most serious complications of the serotonin-releasing drugs fenfluramine (the "fen" in "fen-phen") and dexfenfluramine (Redux)—primary pulmonary hypertension (PPH) and heart valve damage—might also occur at an elevated rate among tryptophan and 5-HTP users. Only new studies will assure us, for example, that the sudden death from an apparent pulmonary embolism (a complication of PPH) of an old man with an EMS-like syndrome associated with his use of pre-Showa-Denko tryptophan and 5-HTP was likely just a coincidence, as his doctors supposed (Joly et al., 1991).

But there is some good news, too: the body has ways of handling tryptophan, 5-HTP and their metabolites safely, and we can help it.

The 1 or 2 g of dietary tryptophan most of us consume every day are either incorporated into proteins or metabolized along several other pathways. The major pathways lead to NAD (the active form of vitamin B3) or, to a much, much lesser degree (about 10 mg's worth), to serotonin and these biochemicals' safely excretable breakdown products. Excesses of some of these chemicals—including serotonin itself—can irritate or even damage various tissues and organs. One way such excesses can arise is if the body is short in the coenzymes (vitamin derivatives) and cofactors (certain minerals) required to process them further. A lack of vitamins B6 and C, for example, can lead to a tumor-inducing glut of *3-hydroxyanthranilic acid* in the bladder (Sourkes, 1983).

A generous intake of these supportive nutrients (which are often prescribed with tryptophan) could lessen the metabolic hazards of taking tryptophan and 5-HTP while maximizing their conversion to serotonin and NAD (which can be an antidepressant in its own right). While at this point it's as much guesswork as science, a reasonable protocol might be to try to balance every 500 mg of supplementary tryptophan (and perhaps every 50 mg of 5-HTP) with at least 5 to 10 mg of B6 (up to 50 mg a day, but possibly much less with 5-HTP, as discussed below) or 1 to 2 mg of pyridoxyl-5-phosphate (up to 10 to 15 mg a day—again, possibly much less with 5-HTP), 25 mg of B3, 100 mcg of folic acid, 100 mg of C, 50 IU of E and possibly 50 mg of methionine or SAM. A good diet and a well-endowed multivitamin and mineral supplement can fill much or all of this prescription and round it off with other nutrients (chromium, other essential amino acids) that may also be needed to keep things safely balanced.

However, there are special considerations when it comes to taking vitamin B6 with 5-HTP. If B6 levels are high when 5-HTP is ingested, a potentially harmful excess of serotonin could be synthesized before the 5-HTP has had a chance to enter the brain. This peripheral serotonin cannot enter the brain, and worse, as Steve Harris, M.D., cautions, in excess it theoretically could precipitate some of the dire consequences mentioned above (1996). Some "smart drug" proponents (for example, South, 1997) have fiercely rebutted Harris's warnings, claiming, among other things, that such reactions have never been reported in the hundreds, if not thousands, of people who have taken 5-HTP with high doses of B6. But reactions such as gradual sclerosis of the right heart valve or lungs could have gone unnoticed or unattributed to 5-HTP. Targeted research is needed to settle this concern.

One possible precaution suggested by Harris, would be to take 5-HTP with a drug like *carbidopa* that blocks the peripheral conversion of 5-HTP to serotonin (1996). This is often done in Europe, albeit for efficiency, not safety. Yet, surprisingly, this combination has tended to be slightly less effective—and much less user-friendly—than taking 5-HTP alone (Zmilacher et al., 1988; South, 1997). More to the point—and no less surprising—it seems that all or most of the rare scleroderma-like reactions have occurred in people *taking the combination*. This has prompted some investigators to blame carbidopa, not 5-HTP, for the trouble (Joly et al., 1991). Adding to the ambiguity, in one report an excess of the noxious tryptophan metabolite kynurenine was implicated as the cause, not just in the 5-HTP/carbidopa users, but in other scleroderma sufferers, too (Sternberg et al., 1980). Ironically, B6 is the body's best defense against kynurenine buildup.

Users of 5-HTP would be wise to keep abreast of the latest information on these safety concerns. For now, a prudent middle course might be to keep one's daily intake of B6 adequate (2 to 5 mg a day) or even generous (10 to 15 mg), but not extravagant, while taking 5-HTP, and to take the B6 at a different time of day.

A few other practices may minimize the hazards of using tryptophan and 5-HTP:

- Several amino acids compete with tryptophan and 5-HTP for seats on the macromolecular shuttle that carries them all across the blood-brain barrier (BBB). High-carbohydrate, low-or no-protein meals or snacks cause most of these competing aminos to be swept from the bloodstream—but not tryptophan. Consequently, taking tryptophan (or 5-HTP) long after you've eaten protein (or taken competing amino acid supplements: methionine, phenylalanine, SAM, or tyrosine)—especially if you swallow some high-carbohydrate foods (fruit, grains) first—will give your brain a very big serotonergic bang for your buck.
- To minimize the risk of consuming contaminated products, buy only pharmaceutical-grade tryptophan and 5-HTP or use the seed-extracted 5-HTP sold by some dealers.
- Negative ionizers—portable electronic devices that emit huge quantities of natural, negatively charged air ions—can markedly reduce elevated blood serotonin levels—and lift some people's moods in the process (Norden, 1995; Baumel, 1995, 1997).
- If your doctor is willing, s/he could periodically monitor your blood or urine for excesses of undesirable metabolites of tryptophan (kynurenine, quinolinic acid, serotonin) or 5-HTP (serotonin). Especially if you're taking 5-HTP, s/he could listen to your heart and lungs for any hint of sclerotic damage.

If you're nervous about using tryptophan or 5-HTP, there are other, perhaps less problematic, approaches that may boost brain serotonin: supplements (in roughly descending order of effectiveness: SJW, SAM, methionine, folic acid, vitamin B3, NADH, vitamin B6, lithium, magnesium, chromium, ginkgo biloba); diet (research suggests that high carbohydrate, low/no-protein meals or snacks or, more generally, a low—but adequate—protein, high-carbohydrate diet, should maximize serotonin levels in the brain while minimizing them peripherally); exercise; progesterone; acupuncture; bright light exposure (at least if you're lacking it); and possibly negative air ions (Norden, 1995; Baumel, 1997).

SIDE EFFECTS, CAUTIONS AND CONTRAINDICATIONS

Especially at low to moderate dosages, tryptophan and 5-HTP are very well-tolerated by most users. However, reported side effects include (in roughly descending order of frequency) gastrointestinal upsets (dry mouth, nausea, vomiting, heartburn, constipation, diarrhea), transient drowsiness or lethargy after taking a dose (these are sleeping pills for many people), diuresis, headache, reduced appetite, dizziness or lightheadedness, loss of balance, tremors, blurred vision, abnormal elation, agitation, sexual disinhibition and hostility or aggressiveness. 5-HTP, which has a similar side-effect profile, is more likely than tryptophan to provoke mania or hypomania or to worsen anxiety (van Praag, 1981; Poldinger et al., 1992). The GI effects can be reduced or eliminated by taking the supplements after food or by using hard-to-find enteric-coated capsules of 5-HTP (van Hiele, 1980; van Praag, 1981).

Thomas Sourkes, M.D., recommends a cautious approach in prescribing tryptophan to people who have hypoglycemia (5-HTP, too) or liver disease (1983). To play it safe, Sourkes also recommends against long-term, high-dose supplementation with tryptophan by children and pregnant women, women on estrogens and anyone with a chronic bladder irritation, a shortage of stomach acid, overgrowth of gastrointestinal microorganisms, upper bowel malabsorption or a history of any scleroderma-like condition (5-HTP, too), diabetes or cancer.

As noted in the previous section, when two or more strongly

serotonin-boosting medications are taken together, especially at high doses, the body's serotonin system can be abruptly shifted into toxic overdrive. In theory, high doses of SJW and other natural serotonin boosters like ginkgo biloba, SAM or methionine might also belong on the list of serotonin boosters to avoid or use cautiously when taking tryptophan or 5-HTP. In practice, some clinicians still mix serotonergic drugs with tryptophan or 5-HTP because the combos can work wonders for some patients and have a good safety record when administered vigilantly (Young, 1991).

TYROSINE AND PHENYLALANINE: TONICS FOR THE BLUE AND WEARY

In their own way, animals get depressed, too. Indeed, some psychologists routinely create "animal models" of depression by subjecting their poor captives to unpredictable, uncontrollable onslaughts of electric shocks or other stressors until the creatures withdraw, broken and defeated, into a shell of "learned helplessness."

Coping with chronic stress, whether you're a mistreated puppy in a psych lab or a panicky yuppy in a bear market, costs chemicals. One of the most important of these is the neurotransmitter *norepinephrine* (NE). Not only does stress crank up the brain's expenditure of NE, eventually it depletes it, along with the puppy's or yuppy's ability to keep on keepin' on.

TYROSINE

It could be a different story if these NE-deprived stress warriors were to take some extra tyrosine. Tyrosine is the amino acid that NE is made from. In some studies, tyrosine has been given to harried lab animals, and the critters have kept on ticking almost as serenely as controls under no stress at all (Salter, 1989).

Is there a lesson here for humans? Army Major Charles A. Salter thinks there is. In preliminary research, tyrosine helped troops bear up better under cold and high-altitude stress. Salter therefore speculates that "dietary supplementation with TYR [tyrosine] . . . may prove to be a simple, safe, and inexpensive way to help troops cope with stress."

Is there a lesson here for depressives?

NE is more than just a stress-buster. It also helps stimulate the so-called "pleasure centers" of the brain, the nerve centers for our Hallmark Moments of pleasure and fulfillment. Thus, low NE could help account for *anhedonia* (lack of pleasure response), one of the defining features of clinical depression. And while NE is by no means the only chemical our happiness depends upon, NE deficiency has long been the main contender (along with serotonin deficiency) for the title of "chemical imbalance most likely to account for depression." Indeed, boosting NE is rivaled only by boosting serotonin as a treatment for depression.

But that's not all. Tyrosine is also the precursor to the dynamic neurotransmitter *dopamine* and to the sparkplug hormones of the thyroid gland (which, in deficiency, likely contribute to 10 to 15 percent of all depressions [Baumel, 1995]), not to mention the fleet-footed hormomes of the adrenal cortex, adrenalin and noradrenaline (also known as norepinephrine).

With such a rich antidepressant resumé in its favor, it should come as no surprise that among doctors who prescribe supplements, tyrosine is both a popular first-line treatment for depression and a trusty last resort (Slagle, 1987; Hendler, 1989; Weil, 1995; Murray, 1996; Braverman et al., 1997). In one practice, an elderly man's 13-year bout of recurrent winter depressions refused to yield to anything—not drugs, not supplements, not Florida—until tyrosine (Braverman et al., 1997).

This has been shown with clinical studies, as well. Details of tyrosine's first modest trial as an antidepressant are unpublished, but the researcher considered it a failure (Coppen 1970). Years later, several Ivy League psychiatrists presented compelling evidence that tyrosine could be just the thing for some depressives. Under double-blind conditions, their chronically depressed patient recovered completely on a large dose of tyrosine, only to relapse on placebo, then recover again on tyrosine (Gelenberg et al., 1980). That same year, another psychiatrist found that the amino acid enabled two of his patients to quit or cut down on the amphetamines that had relieved their depression (Goldberg, 1980). The Harvard collaborators next conducted a small, double-blind, placebo-controlled trial in which tyrosine performed as well as drugs normally do (Gelenberg et al., 1982/83). Finally, in a much larger follow-up study involving 63 patients, they reported that after 4 weeks depressives on the tricyclic antidepressant imipramine enjoyed a 50 percent decrease in symptoms; those on tyrosine, 45 percent; and those on placebo, 35 percent. Had the study lasted longer, the gap between tyrosine and placebo would likely have reached statistical significance, that is, 20 to 1 odds that the gap was real.

Meanwhile, in placebo-controlled studies by Herman van Praag and associates at the Albert Einstein College of Medicine in the Bronx, tyrosine hastened and improved some depressed patients' responses to 5-HTP while rekindling the antidepressant response in others for whom 5-HTP had "pooped out" (1984). Finally, some French psychiatrists have reported that tyrosine is a rapid antidote for what they term "dopamine-dependent depression"—a very sluggish depression with certain signs and symptoms reminiscent of Parkinson's disease and narcolepsy (Mouret et al., 1988).

PHENYLALANINE

Tyrosine itself has a precursor, the amino acid phenylalanine (PA). Although there is evidence that PA doesn't convert too readily to tyrosine in acutely depressed persons (Anderson et al., 1994), PA has other antidepressant tricks up its sleeve. It (and tyrosine) is a building block for many neuropeptides (small brain proteins) implicated in mood control; one form of PA, D-phenylalanine (DPA), inhibits the breakdown of the feel-good neuropeptides known as endorphins; and much of the body's PA is converted into an amphetaminelike neurochemical named *2-phenylethylamine* (PEA). For reasons such as these both forms of PA—the natural "L" form (L-phenylalanine, or LPA) and the synthetic DPA found in DL-phenylalanine (DLPA) supplements—have carved a unique niche for themselves in the (more or less) natural treatment of depression.

DL-PHENYLALANINE

A prominent biological psychiatrist once devoted an entire book to the idea that PEA is the brain's love molecule, its natural amphetamine, the ebullient neuromodulator that makes us giddy when we fall in love, elated when we win a lottery (Liebowitz, 1983). Since the late 1960s, psychiatrists have also hypothesized that a deficiency of this amphetamine-like releaser of dopamine and NE in the brain may be a major cause of depression (Wolf and Mosnaim, 1983; Sabelli et al., 1986). It's not just that there is evidence of a lack of PEA in the bodies of depressives. In all but one of about half a dozen clinical studies, low doses of PEA-boosting DPA and DLPA have proven remarkably effective for hundreds of patients suffering from all kinds and degrees of depression (Beckmann, 1983; Fox and Fox, 1985). In one incredible study, roughly 90 percent of 417 mostly "endogenous" ("chemical imbalance"-type) depressives recovered within two months on DPA. Most of their improvement occurred in the first two weeks. In other studies, DPA and DLPA equaled or bettered relatively low doses of the tricyclic antidepressant imipramine. However, in what seems to be the only completely independent trial, DPA worked for just 2 out of 11 patients—and two others actually deteriorated (Mann, 1980).

Recently, very low doses of PEA itself (10 to 60 mg/day), taken with the MAO-B inhibitor L-deprenyl to impede its breakdown, relieved depression as rapidly as amphetamines (very fast) in 60 percent of the patients (Sabelli et al., 1996).

Many nutritionally oriented practitioners prescribe DLPA for depression (DPA and PEA are unavailable as drugs or supplements). One doctor has written a book on the prescription (Fox and Fox, 1985); and natural health superguru Andrew Weil, M.D., made DLPA his antidepressant supplement of choice in a 1995 bestseller (1995).

L-PHENYLALANINE

L-phenylalanine's vocation for mood-lifting was first revealed in 1966 when an intravenous drip of the amino acid lifted the spirits of patients with Parkinson's disease (Kravitz et al., 1984). Twenty years later, researchers came back for a second look. A very low oral dose of LPA (250 mg/day) sparked recovery or improvement in over 80 percent of 155 depressives who hadn't responded to the weak antidepressant L-deprenyl (Birkmayer et al., 1984). That same year, very large doses of LPA (up to 14 g/day) together with 200 mg/day of vitamin B6 were administered to 40 depressed patients at Rush-Presbyterian-St. Luke's Medical Center in Chicago. Though most of these patients had previously been treatment-resistant, 11 recovered completely on LPA, 20 improved substantially and 2 were bouyed to the point of hypomania (Kravitz et al., 1984; Sabelli et al., 1986). Another psychiatrist soon reported that a low dose of LPA quickly ended the depression of one in every two bipolar patients (Simonson, 1985). More recently, 10 patients with severe, intractable depression were treated to a cocktail of low dose L-deprenyl (5 mg), vitamin B6 (100 mg) and LPA (2 to 6 g/day). "Nine of 10 patients experienced mood elevation within hours of phenylalanine administration," their psychiatrist wrote, "and 6 viewed their episodes of depression as terminated within 2 to 3 days" (Sabelli, 1991).

LPA has found its way into the antidepressant arsenal of many nutritionally oriented practitioners (Slagle, 1987; Weil, 1995; Braverman et al., 1997). Eric Braverman M.D. and associates (1997) found it was just the thing for an emotionally flat, treatment-resistant patient: "Her normal personality returned . . . and she developed once again a normal range of emotions." LPA has been my own staunchest natural shield against depression since I discovered it in 1981.

ARE TYROSINE AND PHENYLALANINE FOR YOU?

Research suggests any depressive is a candidate for tyrosine or PA, but these aminos' stimulating effect may be especially apt for depressions of a sluggish, apathetic persuasion. Bipolars typically suffer such episodes, though, unfortunately, tyrosine and PA often stimulate them into the manic range. A side order of stabilizing tryptophan may be indicated. Ditto for depressives with other excitable conditions, such as anxiety disorders, dyskinesias, poor impulse control, psychosis, seizures and tics. Curiously, Tourette syndrome, which should also belong in this group, is associated with *low* levels of NE, PA, and PEA—only their dopamine is high.

USING TYROSINE AND PHENYLALANINE

A dosage of 100 mg/kg of tyrosine—about 6 to 8 grams for the average adult—has been the norm in studies. But in practice, much lower doses—1 to 6 g/day—have usually sufficed (Slagle, 1987; Braverman et al., 1997).

Surprisingly low doses of DPA and DLPA have been used in the clinical trials. One study suggests these doses—roughly 200 to 600 mg/day of DLPA or its equivalent—can dramatically boost PEA (Fox and Fox, 1985). Yet, in practice, much larger doses are usually prescribed: about 750 to 1500 mg of DLPA in the morning (Weil, 1995) or in divided doses (Fox and Fox, 1985).

LPA seems effective across a very wide dose range—from 250 mg/day (with L-deprenyl, probably higher without) on up, in some studies, to a dozen or more grams a day. The low doses boost PEA, but it's unclear whether the higher doses also increase NE and dopamine or, unexpectedly, decrease them. For whatever reason, depressives usually seem to respond to between 500 mg/day and 6 g/day of LPA (Slagle, 1987; Braverman et al., 1997).

As with tryptophan and 5-HTP, taking these amino acids on a low/no-protein, high-carbohydrate stomach will provide your brain with maximum bang for minimal buck.

People often improve within a few days to a week or two on DLPA and PA. Tyrosine tends to yield slower results. Interestingly, in one small study most depressives didn't relapse after they quit taking DPA or DLPA very soon after responding to it (Yaryura-Tobias, 1978). Similarly, Arnold Fox, M.D. has his patients discontinue DLPA after they've been well for a week and resume only if symptoms return (1985).

ADJUNCTIVE SUPPLEMENTS

Much the same cast of characters that metabolize tryptophan and 5-HTP do likewise for tyrosine and PA (in roughly descending order of importance): folic acid, vitamins B3, B6 and C, SAM, copper, iron, and perhaps other substances. As noted, a good diet and a multivitamin and mineral supplement will help supply these nutrients. Again, too much B6—while not thought to be a toxic concern here—could bolster dopamine and NE synthesis outside the brain countertherapeutically. It's been known to do this in Parkinson's patients taking the dopamine precursor L-dopa. Reportedly, it's also happened to some people taking tyrosine for depression (Mouret et al., 1988). This may be why in one trial where a very high dose of B6 was administered—200 mg/day—the patients needed as much as 14 g/day of LPA (Sabelli et al., 1986). As with tryptophan and 5-HTP, a moderate intake of B6—perhaps no more than 25 to 50 mg, taken apart from the amino acids—may be best.

Some people may benefit from balancing the amino acids they're taking with carefully weighed doses of those they're not. Because these amino acids all compete for passage across the blood-brain barrier and for the attention of key enzymes, high doses of some (especially if taken often each day) could counterproductively reduce brain levels of the neurotransmitters made from the others. A "wired" reaction to tyrosine or PA, for instance, could be due to an induced shortage of soothing serotonin. High doses of these (or any other) amino acids on a low-protein diet could also potentially "induce" a relative deficiency of other amino acids.

SAFETY, SIDE EFFECTS, CAUTION AND CONTRAINDICATIONS

Tyrosine and PA are usually very well-tolerated. Occasional side effects include irritability, aggression, feeling anxious, tense, or "wired," headaches, constipation, nausea or upset stomach, difficulty falling asleep if taken in the evening, mania or hypomania. One man experienced a suicidally depressive crash after enjoying a rapid euphoric reaction to LPA—on two separate occasions (idclub [Internet user name], 1997). Depression, possibly (but not likely) due to the sweetener aspartame's 40 percent LPA content, has been reported by some aspartame users, among many other adverse reactions, including blurred vision, dizziness, and seizures.

Use these supplements cautiously if you have the "excitable" conditions mentioned earlier or cardiac arrythmia,, high blood pressure (PA may raise it; tyrosine will more likely lower it), melanoma, migraines or mitral valve prolapse. Avoid PA if you have phenylketonuria or are pregnant—your fetus could be phenylketonuric. Except perhaps at low doses, tyrosine and PA are no-no's for people on most MAOI drugs and should also be used with caution with herbal MAOIs like ginkgo biloba and SJW.

SAM & CO.: THE METHYLATION MAFIA MAKES SHORT WORK OF MELANCHOLIA

This is probably the first time you're learning about SAM (s-adenosylmethionine, also known as SAMe), even though in Italy this natural biochemical has been commonly prescribed for depression for years.

S-ADENOSYLMETHIONINE (SAM, SAMe)

SAM's antidepressant effect was first reported in Italy in 1973, and it's largely from there that nearly 40 clinical trials (25 of them controlled) involving over a thousand patients have usually affirmed SAM's marked superiority to placebo and its equivalence, if not superiority, to drugs (Bressa, 1994).

Some of America's research elite have put SAM through its paces, too (for example, Kagan et al., 1990; Rosenbaum et al., 1990). And in a psychiatry textbook, the chief of biological psychiatry at the National Institute of Mental Health has admiringly cited "the rapid onset of effects of SAM in a high percentage of patients and the relative absence of side effects in a large number of controlled studies" (Post, 1995).

Actually SAM may not be *that* good unless you inject it every day. The minority of studies using oral SAM suggest it may "only" be as fast and effective as oral drugs for mildly to severely depressed patients. In pill form, SAM has, in fact, performed rather unimpressively in some studies, yielding in one a paltry 22 percent average improvement in self-rated depression (De Vanna and Rigamonti, 1992) and failing in another to significantly better placebo (Fava et al., 1992), though the Harvard investigators suspected a bioavailability problem with the new formulation they used. But every effective antidepressant has its bad days, and overall SAM looks to be the real McCoy. On a good day, in a randomized, double-blind trial from UCLA, six out of nine hospitalized depressives responded to oral SAM after just 3 weeks, compared with one out of six on placebo (Kagan et al., 1990). Though usually very brief, the average controlled trial has found oral SAM to be markedly effective for about half of the depressives studied (Bressa, 1994).

THE SECRET OF SAM'S SUCCESS: *METHYLATION*

One of the more important metabolic processes in the body, methylation refers to the transfer of a very basic biochemical unit known as a methyl group from a methyl donor, like SAM, to a methyl-hungry receiver. In the brain, this transaction can result in anything from the transformation of an amino acid into a neurotransmitter to the rejuvenation of the receptors on a neuron. Indeed, all the major neurotransmitters that tend to be scarce in depression—dopamine, NE, serotonin—need SAM for their synthesis. And while they also need it for their breakdown, SAM's net effect, research suggests, is to boost serotonin and possibly dopamine, and NE, too (Young, 1993).

Though SAM is the brain's principal methyl donor, it couldn't do its handiwork without two key lieutenants: the essential dietary amino acid methionine and the B vitamin folic acid. Here's how it works: SAM is made from methionine. Whenever SAM donates its methyl group, it becomes S-adenosylhomocysteine, then homocysteine. The homocysteine (which can promote cardiovascular disease) is summarily remethylated to methionine by another important methyl donor derived from folic acid: 5-methyl-tetrahydrofolate—methylfolate for short. Thus, SAM and its dietary precursor methionine, and methylfolate and its dietary precursor folic acid, are the mainstays of the brain's methylation mafia. And they all, it seems, can be antidepressants.

METHIONINE

Which is good, because SAM alone ain't nickel and dime. In 1998, a contract for SAM to take out your depression would likely cost you $5 or $10 a day. Yet, over at the corner health food store, lean, mean, hungry methionine would do the same job (or at least try) for just a few bits a day.

Methionine may actually be more than just a cheap SAM substitute. In animals, it actually appears to cross the blood-brain barrier and raise brain levels of SAM better than SAM, gram for gram (Braverman et al., 1997). And while depressives tend to convert methionine to SAM rather sluggishly, some researchers still see methionine as an antidepressant contender (Lipinski, 1986; Young, 1993). Others have already found this to be so. Years ago orthomolecular psychiatrist Dr. Carl Pfeiffer noted that a subgroup of depressives and depressed schizophrenics who typically have high blood levels of histamine, high allergic reactivity (hay fever, and the like), and obsessive and suicidal tendencies usually benefit from methionine (which lowers histamine). One patient liberated by methionine "felt as if he had been in a concentration camp for the last seven years" (Braverman et al., 1997).

FOLIC ACID (FOLATE, FOLACIN)

Of the many nutritional deficiencies that depressives are heir to (Baumel, 1995), none is as prevalent as folic acid deficiency (Young, 1993; Alpert and Fava, 1997). In most investigations, roughly 15 to 40 percent of depressives have had it to some degree, and the deeper the depression, the deeper the folate deficiency. In contrast, depressives with high blood levels of folate have tended to suffer briefer depressions and shorter hospitalizations and to respond better to antidepressant drugs. And recovered depressives with high folate levels have suffered fewer setbacks.

Physiologically, folate deficiency begets SAM deficiency and a deficiency of another important catalyst: tetrahydrobiopterin (BH4). Not only does BH4 help catalyze the synthesis of dopamine, NE and serotonin, it also stimulates neurons to release them. It's enough to make experts suspect that folate deficiency is more than just a sign of malnutrition among people too depressed to eat well (or at all). Some suspect it's a primary cause of depression or a vicious cycle contributor, resulting from the poor diet and/or the stress (stress depletes folate) so commonly associated with depression (Abou-Saleh and Cooper, 1986).

When researchers have administered folate or methylfolate to folate-deficient neuropsychiatric patients, the results have been rewarding: better social functioning, improved mood, relief of mental impairments and gastrointestinal symptoms and shorter hospital stays. (Most of the many folate studies cited in this section are reviewed by Young [1993] and Alpert and Fava [1997].) In one uncontrolled study, an ample dose of folate very gradually brought improvement to 43 out of 50 patients with a chronic syndrome of depression, fatigue, gastrointestinal disturbances, malabsorption and mental impairment.

Some researchers have gone further, prescribing these nutrients to depressives regardless of their folate status. In one double-blind, placebo-controlled study from the British Medical Research Council, recovered depressives on lithium were given a very modest supplement of folic acid (200 mcg/day—half the RDA). After a year, those whose blood-levels had soared high above average (13 ng/ml or above) had suffered 40 percent less symptomatic flare-ups than the others. In follow-up studies, this reduction in "affective morbidity" due to folate or methylfolate has usually been replicated.

In three clinical trials, megadoses of methylfolate (not available commercially in 1998) have also proven to be antidepressants. In one double-blind trial, methylfolate was as effective as amitriptyline, a popular tricyclic antidepressant drug. Patients whose red blood cell levels of methylfolate rose the most improved the most.

Anecdotally, folic acid has long had a place in the antidepressant arsenal of orthomolecular (natural biochemical-oriented) psychiatrists. "I have certainly seen cases where supplementing folic acid up to 20 milligrams per day ended symptoms entirely. . . . The glow of health returns!" one wrote in 1980 (Kunin). Herbert Newbold (1975) has observed that megadoses stimulate some patients, while they sedate others; they make some people feel great, but others feel "just rotten" (especially schizophrenics). For one depressed bipolar patient, nothing worked until his open-minded psychiatrist—Dr. Jambur Ananth, Director of the Psychopharmacology Unit at Harbor-UCLA Medical Center—gambled on a megadose of folate (1986).

IS THE METHYLATION MAFIA FOR YOU?

Research suggests that "retarded" depressions marked by apathy, guilt, lethargy, and suicidal impulses may be most responsive to SAM or methionine. Bipolar people, who typically suffer from lethargic depressions, are highly and rapidly responsive to SAM, often to the point of hypomania. Experimentally, megadoses of methionine (around 20 g/day) have worsened the psychosis of many schizophrenics.

Several depression-related conditions may also be responsive to SAM (and probably methionine): dementia, drug dependency, fibromyalgia, migraine, osteoarthritis and other chronic pain conditions, Parkinson's disease and premenstrual syndrome.

Severe depression and failure to respond to treatment are very strong hints of an underlying folate deficiency (Alpert and Fava, 1997). Other important risk factors include being a teenager or a senior, dementia (including AIDS dementia), heavy drinking, pregnancy, rheumatoid arthritis, and skimping on green vegetables, legumes, organ meats, or oranges and taking anticonvulsants or certain other drugs (including antibiotics, anticancer preparations, cholestyramine and oral contraceptives).

Red blood cell levels of folate are a more reliable gauge of deficiency than serum levels, but some people may only have low CSF levels, indicative of a localized brain deficiency.

USING SAM, METHIONINE AND FOLIC ACID

SAM has been administered orally at a dosage of 1600 mg/day in seven out of eight clinical trials (Bressa, 1994), though some researchers wonder if higher doses would work better (for example, Kagan et al., 1990). Orthomolecular experts find 1 to 2 g/day of methionine to be optimal (Braverman et al., 1997).

An increased intake of SAM/methionine increases the body's need for calcium, folic acid, magnesium, vitamins B6, B12 and C and possibly other nutrients. A good diet and modest supplementation should fill this need.

While doses of folate and methylfolate as low as a few hundred micrograms and as high as 100 mg (250 times the RDA) have been used to treat depression, 1 or 2 mg to a few dozen a day would seem the best bet for safety and efficacy. Extremely high doses can, paradoxically, lower serotonin instead of raise it. This could be the basis for folate's apparent therapeutic window (Albert and Fava, 1997) as well as the occasional adverse psychiatric reaction. The therapeutic window can "descend" with time, necessitating a lower dosage to maintain response (Newbold, 1975). Folate supplements sometimes take months to work.

SAFETY, SIDE EFFECTS, CAUTIONS AND CONTRAINDICATIONS

SAM's side effects are hard to distinguish from those of a placebo (e.g., Kagan et al., 1990). Methionine, too, seems very well-tolerated (Braverman et al., 1997). There is one glaring exception. Bipolar users—and some unipolars—very often become manic or hypomanic on SAM, though the reaction usually passes despite continued use (e.g., Kagan et al., 1990). Other real or apparent side effects reported by users of SAM typically are short-lived, too: anxiety, blurred vision, difficulty urinating, dry mouth, nausea, restlessness, sweating and thirst. Little is known about methionine's side effects, though flatulence and "uneasy feelings" have been reported (Braverman et al., 1997).

Injections of SAM triggered a serotonin syndrome in a woman taking the strong SRI Anafranil (Iruela et al., 1993). Oral SAM (and methionine) in more than minimal, "balancing doses" should therefore be used cautiously, if at all, with other strong serotonergic drugs and possibly lithium, SJW, tryptophan and 5-HTP.

Are there any long-term hazards? In one animal study, a lifetime of severe methionine *restriction* stunted rats' growth dramatically, but it increased their lifespans 30 percent (Orentreich et al., 1993). Some researchers speculate that excessive methylation by SAM may be a causative factor in Parkinson's disease (Charlton and Mack, 1994). Hopefully, the relatively modest amounts of SAM and methionine used to treat depression (diet itself provides about the same amount), if balanced protectively with related nutrients, will have only healthful consequences.

Usually after weeks or months on fairly high doses of folate, some people have become abnormally euphoric or agitated: restless, sleepless, rambunctious, aggressive. Other side effects include abnormal taste, an apparent allergic reaction to folate (fever, flushing, hives, itching, pain), depression, gastrointestional disturbances, malaise and weight loss.

Reportedly, the same depressive, obsessive, suicidal, and allergically reactive schizophrenics who benefit from methionine are usually worsened by folic acid (Braverman et al., 1997). Even though there is disputed evidence that too much folate can provoke seizures (Newbold, 1975), correcting anticonvulsant-induced folate deficiencies has greatly benefited depressed, mentally impaired epileptics in some studies.

Crude hematological screening tests for vitamin B12 deficiency are unreliable if you're taking a folate supplement. Folic acid supplements may slightly impair zinc absorption, but a good diet and multivitamin and mineral supplement should compensate.

COMBINING ANTIDEPRESSANTS: PROMISES AND PERILS

That two or more antidepressants, taken together, can accomplish much more than either one alone is well-documented. A low dose of thyroid hormone or lithium, for instance, converts about 50 percent of antidepressant drug nonresponders into responders. And so, research suggests, can adjunctive phenylalanine, SAM or tryptophan. Combination therapies can also work faster and better than monotherapies from the start. But if these combinations can be therapeutically synergistic, so too can they be synergistically hazardous.

So far, these hazards have only seemed to occur where two antidepressants that strongly boost a neurotransmitter or other chemical via *different* mechanisms have been combined. MAOI drugs, for instance, inhibit the breakdown of serotonin, tyramine, and other amines. Combine them with drugs that block the "reuptake" (reabsorption) of serotonin into the neurons that secrete it or with amino acid precursors to serotonin or the "pressor" amine tryptamine, and you have the makings of a potentially deadly serotonin syndrome or hypertensive crisis.

Among natural antidepressants, there are combinations which, in theory, belong to this gifted but dysfunctional family. Because SJW shows signs of being a mild MAOI and an inhibitor of serotonin and norepinephrine reuptake, it could be very unpleasant or dangerous for some people to combine it with methionine, phenylalanine, SAM, tryptophan, 5-HTP, tyrosine or maybe even folic acid (though I doubt it). But it also could prove highly therapeutic. Certainly, relatively low doses of combined ingredients are least likely to trigger adverse interactions. Used carefully, such combinations could be the safest and most effective solution for many people's depression.

Fortunately, combining antidepressants which boost *different* neurotransmitters doesn't seem to create any synergistically toxic surprises. Most antidepressant drugs do this inherently. The classic MAOIs and tricyclics and the newer drug venlafaxine all simultaneously boost NE and serotonin (not to mention PEA) to varying degrees. The natural equivalent would be to combine a serotonin precursor (tryptophan or 5-HTP) with an NE precursor (tyrosine or, maybe, phenylalanine) and a PEA precursor (DLPA or LPA). Orthomolecular practitioners often prescribe such combinations, sometimes with drugs, using their patients' symptoms, clinical reactions and blood monitoring (in some clinics) as a guide (for example, Slagle, 1987; Murray, 1996). What little research there is confirms the therapeutic edge such combinations can provide (van Praag, 1984).

One Man's Experience

On their own or under professional care, many people are experimenting with combinations of natural antidepressants, sometimes in combination with small doses of antidepressant drugs. "I personally take L-tyrosine (500 mg) with B6 and vitamin C in the morning, with two St. John's Wort pills (300 mg, 0.3 hypericin) and L-tryptophan (500 mg) in the evening," writes one depressive (Internet user name "nun," 1997). "I feel energetic and a sense of well being I haven't felt in a long time. I tried each of them separately and they gave some relief, but [they] only worked for a while and not as good as the combo. This may be a dangerous combo, but I have had no problems yet."

If you find a balance of supplements or a single supplement that works for you, how long should you take it? If you've recovered from a lengthy and severe depression, studies of antidepressant drugs would suggest that you're likely to relapse within a few months if you stop taking them. So you probably shouldn't quit or cut down sharply until you've been well for at least a few months. If you've suffered from very chronic or frequent depressions, or if your life circumstances put you at continuing risk for depression, it may be necessary to fortify yourself indefinitely, with lower doses, perhaps, in good times.

But what if these natural antidepressants haven't worked for you? Or what if they have, but you'd rather not keep putting them into your body? If that's the case, other natural approaches may serve you better.

ALTERNATIVE ALTERNATIVES: MORE NATURAL ANTIDEPRESSANTS TO THE RESCUE

Depression is a total mind-body experience that engulfs a person, head to toe, "sole to soul." It's not surprising that this malaise should be approachable from so many different therapeutic angles: drugs, nutrients, psychotherapy. When it comes to natural antidepressant interventions, some books have covered far more than I have in this slim volume (see, for example, Slagle, 1987; Baumel, 1995; Norden, 1995; Murray, 1996). But in this section I can at least give you the lay of the land.

To begin with, take good old-fashioned psychotherapy. Research has proven it to be as effective as any other antidepressant for all, perhaps, but severe bipolar, melancholic or psychotic (delusional or hallucinatory) depression. But not just any kind of psychotherapy will do. Only a few have proven widely helpful. At the forefront is *cognitive therapy* (see, for example, Burns, 1980) and other cognitive-behavioral approaches which focus on teaching people to take more control of their depressing thoughts and to increase their daily participation in rewarding activities. Focused, short-term, problem-oriented counseling in the form of *interpersonal psychotherapy* has also performed quite well in controlled clinical trials. Anecdotally, many depressives draw strength from support groups.

The feel-good effect of exercise is common knowledge, but regular exercise also has a clinically significant antidepressant effect, even in hospitalized patients. At the opposite extreme, deep relaxation—particularly meditation—can gradually relieve depression, too, especially perhaps where chronic stress is at the heart of it.

On the nutritional front, several nutritional imbalances are implicated as causes of depression: too much saturated or hydrogenated fats, not enough fresh unsaturated fats and oils, especially those rich in omega-3 fatty acids (such as flax/linseed oil, fatty cold-water fish and seafood); too much sodium, not enough potassium and possibly (especially for bipolar disorder) too much calcium, not enough magnesium; and too much refined carbohydrates, not enough fiber-rich complex carbohydrates. Nutrient deficiencies are rife in depression, especially of the B vitamins, but also of vitamin C, magnesium, zinc and probably others. "Megadose" supplements of nutrients not featured in this book (acetylcarnitine, B1, B6, B12, C, NADH, niacin, inositol,) and moderate doses of calcium, magnesium and zinc have been found—anecdotally and in some clinical studies—to be antidepressants for some people. Not only do high doses of lithium (a naturally ubiquitous mineral that may be a nutrient) allay bipolar disorder, but they are a well-established adjunct and maintenance therapy for "unipolar" depression, too.

St. John's Wort is not the only herbal antidepressant; it's just the only one that's supported by droves of studies. Others include damiana, ginkgo biloba, ginseng, oat extract and scullcap. A dash of thyroid is a proven "augmentor" of antidepressant drugs. There is growing evidence that aromatherapy can lift moods and relieve depression. Homeopathy is a popular, if controversial, alternative medical approach which has usually worked for many conditions, including depression, in a large body of controlled trials.

Bright light is the treatment of choice for the recurrent fall/winter depression form of seasonal affective disorder (SAD). Studies also indicate it can help relieve nonseasonal depression, too, especially lethargic, SAD-type depression. Properly timed, bright light can bring depressives' disturbed sleep-wake and body rhythm cycles back into synch, easing their depression in the process. So can directly time-shifting their sleep-wake schedules. Not sleeping at all for a night, or skipping the last half of one's bedtime, is a little known but well-established acute antidepressant. Though the relief seldom lasts, when combined with slower acting antidepressants, the result can indeed be "lasting overnight relief" from depression. For burned out or chronically sleep-deprived depressives, sleeping or napping more can be the ticket.

Massage and other forms of bodywork such as *hatha yoga* and *t'ai chi* can also relieve depression. Daily acupuncture has even proven as effective as drugs in hospitalized depressives.

Mental imagery and verbal suggestions or affirmations can be used to counteract or neutralize the depressive process. Making or partaking of the creative arts—dance, journaling, music and so on—can help one "work through" the emotional knots that foster depression or work one's way out of the pit itself.

Many medically well-established conditions can masquerade as depression or promote it: diabetes, hypothyroidism, toxic depressive reactions to drugs or home or workplace chemicals. Other controversial conditions appear to do likewise: "brain allergies" to commonly eaten foods or environmental chemicals, chronic overexposure to magnetic fields from electrical appliances, chronic systemic yeast infection (the "Candida syndrome"), mercury poisoning from amalgam ("silver") dental fillings, positive air-ion overload and reactive hypoglycemia (low blood sugar).

There are many, many ways to get depressed. But, thankfully, there are almost as many ways to get over it.

RESOURCES: WHERE TO FIND NATURAL ANTIDEPRESSANTS

All the natural antidepressants discussed in this book are currently available wherever nutritional supplements are sold—with a few exceptions:

- Single amino acids are unavailable over the counter in Canada. But they can be legally ordered or imported from the United States for personal use. *Tryptan* (tryptophan) is available in Canada by prescription. Americans can also obtain tryptophan by prescription from compounding pharmacies. A very few suppliers offer tryptophan without a prescription (see below).

- Carbidopa is available only by prescription from some compounding pharmacies.
- SAM is very expensive and very hard to find.

Here are some sellers of hard-to-find supplements:

- BIOS Biochemicals (520-326-7610; <www.biochemicals.com>) and England's International Antiaging Systems (IAS) (011-44-541-51-4144; <www.smart-drugs.com>) sell tryptophan without a prescription.
- The Life Extension Foundation (800-841-5433; <www.lef.org>) and IAS are two sellers of SAM.
- Medical Center Pharmacy (800-723-7455) is a compounding pharmacy that sells tryptophan and carbidopa by prescription.
- Among the many mail-order companies from whom Canadians and Americans can buy amino acids, 5-HTP and (in some cases) NADH and pyridoxyl-5-phosphate are BIOS, IAS, Swanson Health Products (800-437-4148, <www.swansonsvitamins.com>). The Vitamin Shoppe (800-223-1216; <www.vitaminshoppe.com>) and Vitamin Research Products (800-877-2447; <www.vrp.com>).

REFERENCES

Abou-Saleh, M. T., and A. Coppen, "The Biology of Folate in Depression: Implications for Nutritional Hypotheses of the Psychoses," *Journal of Psychiatric Research* 20 (2, 1986): 91–101.

Alpert, J. E., and M. Fava, "Nutrition and Depression: The Role of Folate," *Nutrition Reviews*, 55 (May 1997) :145–49.

Ananth, Jambur, letter to the author, May 1986.

Anderson, D. N., et al., "Recovery from Depression After Electroconvulsive Therapy Is Accompanied by Evidence of Increased Tetrahydrobiopterin-dependent Hydroxylation," *Acta Psychiatrica Scandinavica*, 90 (July 1994): 10–13.

Arneson, Mary, "Regulatory Weakness Cost 'Grandma' the Use of Her Right Side, and I'd Like to Know Why," *Minneapolis Star-Tribune*, Nov. 19, 1997.

Baumel, Syd, *Dealing With Depression Naturally* (New Canaan, Conn.: Keats Publishing, 1995).

————, *Serotonin: How to Naturally Harness the Power Behind Prozac and Phen/Fen* (New Canaan, Conn.: Keats Publishing, 1997).

Beckmann, H., "Phenylalanine in Affective Disorders," *Advances in Biological Psychiatry* 10 (1983): 137–47.

Birkmayer, W. et al., "L-deprenyl Plus L-phenylalanine in the Treatment of Depression," *Journal of Neural Transmission* 159 (1, 1984): 81–87.

Blauvelt, Andrew, and Vincent Falanga, "Idiopathic and L-Tryptophan-Associated Eosinophilic Fasciitis Before and After L-Tryptophan Contamination," *Archives of Dermatology* 127 (August 1991): 1159–66.

Bloomfield, Harold H., and Peter McWilliams, *Hypericum & Depression* (Los Angeles, Prelude Press, 1997). Also published at www.hypericum.com.

Braverman, Eric R., with Carl C. Pfeiffer, et al., *The Healing Nutrients Within* (New Canaan, Conn.: Keats Publishing, 1997).

Bressa, G. M., "S-Adenosyl-L-Methionine (SAMe) as Antidepressant: Meta-Analysis of Clinical Studies," *Acta Neurologica Scandinavica* 154 (1994, Suppl.): 7–14.

Burns, David, *Feeling Good: The New Mood Therapy* (New York: William Morrow, 1980).

Catterall, W. E., "Tryptophan and Bladder Cancer" (letter), *Biological Psychiatry* 24 (October 1988): 733–34.

Charlton, C. G., and J. Mack, "Substantia Nigra Degeneration and Tyrosine Hydroxylase Depletion Caused by Excess S-Adenosylmethionine in the Rat Brain: Support for an Excess Methylation Hypothesis for Parkinsonism," *Molecular Neurobiology* 9 (August-December 1994): 149–61.

Coppen, A. J., "The Chemical Pathology of the Affective Disorders," in *The Scientific Basis of Medicine Annual Reviews* (London: Athlone Press, 1970), pp. 189–210.

Cracchiolo, Camilla, "FAQ on St. John's Wort," 1997 (<www.primenet.com/~camilla/STJOHNS.FAQ>).

De Vanna, M., and R. Rigamonti, "Oral S-Adenosyl-L-Methionine in Depression," *Current Therapeutic Research* 52 (September 1992): 478–85.

Fava, M., et al., "The Thyrotropin Response to Thyrotropin-Releasing Hormone as a Predictor of Response to Treatment in Depressed Outpatients," *Acta Psychiatrica Scandinavica* 86 (1992): 42–45.

Fox, Arnold, and Barry Fox, *DLPA to End Chronic Pain and Depression* (New York: Pocket Books, 1985).

Gelenberg, Alan J., et al., "Neurotransmitter Precursors for the Treatment of Depression," *Psychopharmacology Bulletin* (January 1982): 7–18.

————, et al., "Tyrosine for Depression," *Journal of Psychiatric Research* 17(2, 1982/83):175–80.

————, et al., "Tyrosine for Depression: A Double-Blind Trial," *Journal of Affective Disorders* 19 (June 1990): 125–32.

————, et al., "Tyrosine for the Treatment of Depression," *American Journal of Psychiatry* 137 (1980): 622–23.

Gold, Mark S., with Lois B. Morris, *The Good News About Depression* (New York: Bantam, 1987).

Goldberg, I. K., "L-tyrosine in Depression," *Lancet* 2 (1980): 364.

Gordon, J. B., "SSRIs and St. John's Wort: Possible Toxicity?" *American Family Physician* 57 (March 1): 950.

Harris, Steven B., "5-HTP + B6 = Trouble; Doc Harris Presents Green Banana Award," sci.med.nutrition (and several other Internet newsgroups), Dec. 28, 1996.

Hendler, Sheldon Saul, *The Oxygen Breakthrough* (New York: William Morrow, 1989).

idclub (Internet user name), "The L-phenylalanine WARNING Continues . . . ," sci.med.psychobiology (and several other Internet newsgroups), Oct. 17, 1997.

Iruela, L. M. et al., "Toxic Interaction of S-Adenosylmethionine and Clomipramine" (letter), *American Journal of Psychiatry* 150 (March 1993): 522.

Joly, P., et al., "Development of Pseudobullous Morphea and Scleroderma-like Illness During Therapy with L-5-Hydroxytryptophan and Carbidopa," *Journal of the American Academy of Dermatology* 25 (August 1991): 332–33.

Kravitz, Howard M., et al., "Dietary Supplements of Phenylalanine and Other Amino Acid Precursors of Brain Neuroamines in the Treatment of Depressive Disorders," *Journal of the American Osteopathic Organization* 84 (September 1984, Suppl.): 119–23.

Kunin, Richard A., *Mega-Nutrition* (New York: McGraw Hill, 1980).

Lam, R. W., et al., "L-tryptophan Augmentation of Light Therapy in Patients with Seasonal Affective Disorder," *Canadian Journal of Psychiatry* 42 (April 1997): 303–06.

Liebowitz, Michael R., *The Chemistry of Love* (New York: Little, Brown, 1983).

Linde, K., et al., "St. John's Wort for Depression: An Overview and Meta-Analysis of Randomised Clinical Trials," *British Medical Journal* 313 (Aug. 3, 1996): 253–58.

Lipinski, Joseph P., letter to the author, 1986.

Mann, John, "D-Phenylalanine in Endogenous Depression," *American Journal of Psychiatry* (December 1980): 1611.

Michelson, D., et al., "An Eosinophilia-Myalgia Syndrome Related Disorder Associated with Exposure to L-5-Hydroxytryptophan," *Journal of Rheumatology* 21 (December 1994): 2261–65.

Moller, S. E., et al., "Relationship Between Plasma Ratio of Tryptophan to Competing Amino Acids and the Response to L-Tryptophan," *Journal of Affective Disorders* 2 (March 1980): 47–59.

Mouret, Jacques, et al., "Treatment of Narcolepsy with L-Tyrosine," *Lancet* (Dec. 24/31, 1988): 1458–59.

Murray, Michael T., *Natural Alternatives to Prozac* (New York: William Morrow, 1996).

Newbold, H. L., *Mega-Nutrients for Your Nerves* (New York: Berkley Books, 1975).

Norden, Michael J., *Beyond Prozac* (New York: HarperCollins, 1995).

Nordfors, M., and P. Hartvig, ["St John's Wort Against Depression in Favour Again"] *Lakartidningen* 94 (June 18, 1997): 2365–67.

nun (Internet user name), "Re: Amino Acids; Feeling of Well-Being ????" misc. health.alternative (an Internet newsgroup), Aug. 5, 1997.

Orentreich, N., et al., "Low Methionine Ingestion by Rats Extends Life Span," *Journal of Nutrition* 123 (February 1993): 269–74.

Poldinger, W., et al., "A Functional-Dimensional Approach to Depression: Serotonin Deficiency as a Target Symptom in a Comparison of 5-Hydroxytryptophan and Fluvoxamine," *Psychopathology* 24 (1991):53–81.

Post, Robert M., "Mood Disorders: Somatic Treatment," eds. In Harold I. Kaplan and

Benjamin J. Sadock, *Comprehensive Textbook of Psychiatry,* Vol. 6 (Baltimore: Williams & Wilkins, 1995), pp. 1152–78.

Rosenbaum, J. F., et al., "The Antidepressant Potential of Oral S-Adenosyl-L-Methionine," *Acta Psychiatrica Scandinavica* 81 (May 1990): 432–36.

Sabelli, H. C., "Rapid Treatment of Depression with Selegiline-Phenylalanine Combination" (letter), *Journal of Clinical Psychiatry* 52 (March 1991): 137.

———, et al., "Clinical Studies on the Phenylalanine Hypothesis of Affective Disorder: Urine and Blood Phenylacetic Acid and Phenylalanine Dietary Supplements," *Journal of Clinical Psychiatry* 47 (February 1986): 66–70.

———, et al., "Sustained Antidepressant Effect of PEA Replacement," *Neuropsychiatry Clinics and Neuroscience* 8 (2, 1996): 168–71.

Salter, Charles A., "Dietary Tyrosine as an Aid to Stress Resistance Among Troops," *Military Medicine* 154 (March 1989): 144–46.

Simonson, M., "L-Phenylalanine" (letter), *Journal of Clinical Psychiatry* 46 (August 1985): 355.

Slagle, Priscilla, *The Way Up from Down* (New York: Random House, 1987).

Sourkes, T. L., "Toxicology of Serotonin Precursors," *Advances in Biological Psychiatry* 10 (1983): 160–75.

South, James, "Controversy Erupts About Safety of 5-HTP," *Nutritional News* 11 (March 1997). Also published at www.vrp.com.

Sternberg, E. M., et al., "Development of a Scleroderma-Like Illness During Therapy with L-5-Hydroxytryptophan and Carbidopa," *New England Journal of Medicine* 303 (Oct. 2, 1980): 782–87.

Van Hiele, L. J., "L-5-Hydroxytryptophan in Depression: The First Substitution Therapy in Psychiatry?" *Neuropsychobiology* 6 (4, 1980): 230–40.

Van Praag, Herman M., "Management of Depression with Serotonin Precursors," *Biological Psychiatry* 16 (3, 1981): 291–310.

———, "Studies in the Mechanism of Action of Serotonin Precursors in Depression," *Psychopharmacology Bulletin* 20 (3, 1984): 599–602.

Vorbach, E. U., et al., "Efficacy and Tolerability of St. John's Wort Extract L1160 versus Imipramine in Patients with Severe Depressive Episodes According to ICD-10," *Pharmacopsychiatry* 30 (September 1997, Suppl.): 81–85.

Weil, Andrew, *Natural Health, Natural Medicine,* rev. ed. (Boston: Houghton Mifflin, 1995).

Wolf, M. E., and A. D. Mosnaim, "Pheylethylamine in Neuropsychiatric Disorders," *General Pharmacology* 14 (4, 1983): 385–90.

Yaryura-Tobias, J. A., "Use of D-Phenylalanine in the Treatment of Depression: Theoretical and Clinical Implications," eds. in A. D. Mosnaim and Marion Wolf, *Noncatecholic Phenylethylamines,* pt. 1 *Phenylethylamine: Biological Mechanisms and Clinical Aspects* (New York: Marcel Dekker, 1978), pp. 489–508.

Young, Simon N., "The Use of Diet and Dietary Components in the Study of Factors Controlling Affect in Humans: A Review," *Journal of Psychiatry and Neuroscience* 18 (November 1993): 235–44.

———, "Use of Tryptophan in Combination with Other Antidepressant Treatments: A Review," *Journal of Psychiatry and Neuroscience* 16 (December 1991): 241–46.

Zmilacher, K., et al., "L-5-Hydroxytryptophan Alone and in Combination with a Peripheral Decarboxylase Inhibitor in the Treatment of Depression," *Neuropsychobiology* 20 (1988): 28–35.